LEVEL
1

George Washington Carver

Kitson Jazynka

NATIONAL
GEOGRAPHIC

Washington, D.C.

For kids who love to discover, learn, and teach, like George Washington Carver did —K. J.

Trade paperback ISBN: 978-1-4263-2285-3
Reinforced library binding ISBN: 978-1-4263-2286-0

Editor: Shelby Alinsky
Art Director: Callie Broaddus
Editorial: Snapdragon Books
Designer: YAY! Design
Photo Editor: Christina Ascani
Special Projects Assistant: Kathryn Williams
Rights Clearance Specialists: Michael Cassady & Mari Robinson
Design Production Assistants: Sanjida Rashid & Rachel Kenny
Manufacturing Manager: Rachel Faulise
Production Editor: Mike O'Connor
Managing Editor: Grace Hill

The publisher and author gratefully acknowledge the expert content review of this book by Paxton J. Williams, Esq., former executive director of the George Washington Carver Birthplace Association, and the literacy review of this book by Mariam Jean Dreher, professor of reading education at the University of Maryland, College Park.

Photo Credits

**National Geographic supports K–12 educators with ELA Common Core Resources.
Visit natgeoed.org/commoncore for more information.**

Printed in the United States of America
15/WOR/1

Table of Contents

Who Was Carver?

George Washington Carver loved studying plants. He showed farmers how to grow sustainable (suh-STANE-uh-bul) crops. That helped them farm better and eat better.

He also found that hundreds of things could be made from peanut plants. Growing peanuts helped farmers earn money.

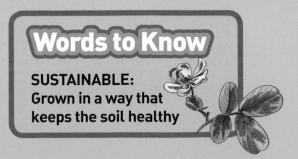

Words to Know

SUSTAINABLE: Grown in a way that keeps the soil healthy

This painting of George Washington Carver was made in 1942.

Many black farmers were too poor to buy their own land. Instead, they had to rent it. They paid the owner a share of their crops.

In Carver's time, life was hard for many black people in the United States. They did not have the same rights as white people.

Carver felt that this was wrong. He used his ideas about farming to help change people's lives.

Carver was one of the most famous African Americans of his time.

Growing Up

The cabin where Carver lived as a boy is gone. This outline (photo above) was built later to show how small it was. This sketch (right) was drawn by Carver. It shows how he remembers the cabin.

George Washington Carver was born on a farm near Diamond, Missouri, U.S.A.

Most people think he was born around 1864. No one knows for sure. But we do know he was born a slave.

Back then, slaves were often given their owner's last name. George's owners were Moses and Susan Carver. So his last name was Carver too.

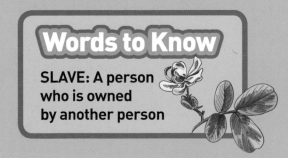

Words to Know

SLAVE: A person who is owned by another person

This statue shows Carver as a boy. It stands at the George Washington Carver National Monument in Diamond, Missouri. This was the first national monument to honor an African American.

One night, men kidnapped baby George Carver and his mother. He was returned to the farm, but his mother was not.

Soon after, slavery ended. Moses and Susan Carver decided to raise George. As a boy, he loved to explore the farm. He collected rocks. He grew a garden. He asked questions.

In His Own Words

"When I talk to the little flower or to the little peanut, they will give up their secrets."

11

In His Time

Carver grew up in the midwestern United States during the 1870s. Back then, many things were different from how they are today.

TRANSPORTATION: Many people traveled on foot, in wagons pulled by horses, or by steamboat or train.

MONEY: Most freed slaves had little or no money. They often traded for things they needed.

FOOD: Few people shopped in stores for food. Instead, they raised farm animals. They also grew fruits and vegetables to feed their families.

SCHOOL: Children went to school in one-room schoolhouses or even old barns.

U.S. EVENTS: In 1872, Ulysses S. Grant was re-elected president of the United States.

TOYS AND FUN: Children spent time outdoors and played with handmade toys.

A Love of Learning

Carver loved to learn. But in his town, black children could not go to school. Carver learned to read at home. He had only one book.

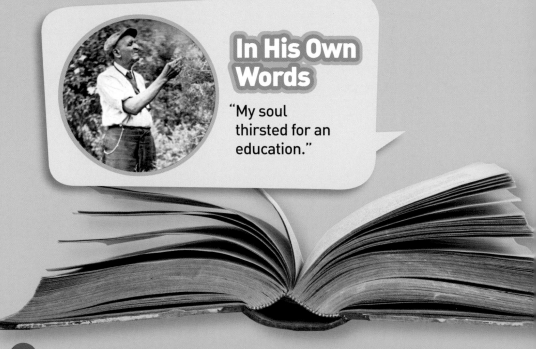

In His Own Words

"My soul thirsted for an education."

This drawing shows a school for black children during Carver's time.

Carver wanted to learn more.
At around age 13, he left home.
He lived with a black family
in a nearby town. There he went
to a school for black children.

Later, Carver wanted to go to college. Many black Americans still faced racism (RAY-siz-um). One school would not let Carver in because he was black.

But he didn't give up. He became the first black student at Iowa State College. He studied agriculture (AG-ri-kul-chur).

Words to Know

RACISM: The belief that one group of people is better than another

AGRICULTURE: The science of farming

In 1894, Carver got his degree from Iowa State College (shown below).

6 COOL FACTS About Carver

1 Carver grew up on a farm with horses, cattle, honeybees, and wheat crops.

2 As a boy, Carver helped people with their sick plants. They called him the "plant doctor."

3 The U.S. Navy named two ships after Carver.

4 Carver added "Washington" to his name because another George Carver lived in his town.

5 Carver loved art. He made paint from berries. He tied twigs together for a brush.

6 Three U.S. presidents asked for Carver's advice on farming.

Carver meeting President Franklin D. Roosevelt in 1939

Helping Others

After college, Carver became a teacher. He worked at a school in Alabama called Tuskegee Institute (tuh-SKEE-gee IN-stuh-toot).

Carver (front row, center) sits with his fellow teachers at Tuskegee Institute.

Carver (second from right) taught in this lab at Tuskegee Institute in 1906.

There he did important work with plants. He found many new ways to use sweet potatoes and soybeans. He invented hundreds of new things, such as paints, plastics, and dyes.

He also wanted to help farmers.
He built a classroom on a wagon.
It was pulled by mules. He drove
the wagon to nearby farms to
teach about agriculture.

This was the first wagon classroom Carver used.

Most farmers couldn't come to Carver's classroom. So Carver wanted to bring his ideas to them.

Carver thought that planting peanuts could help farmers too. Peanut plants would keep the soil healthy.

Carver said a massage with peanut oil could help a sick person. The oil was sold in bottles like these.

Farmers could also sell this crop to earn more money. Carver had found more than 300 ways to use peanut plants. They could be turned into glue, medicine, gasoline, and even paper.

Good Ideas

Carver traveled. He gave speeches about farming. He spoke about peanuts. He also spoke about treating all people fairly.

In 1921, he spoke to the U.S. Congress. Some people in Congress didn't want to listen to a black man. But he had good ideas. Finally Congress listened. They shared his ideas with others.

1864
Born around this year

1865
Slavery ends in the United States

1877
Leaves home to go to school

In His Own Words

"I want to feel that my life has been of some service to my fellow man."

1894

Earns his first degree from Iowa State College

1896

Earns another degree from Iowa State College

Hard Work

Carver died in 1943. He was around 79 years old. Carver's hard work helped many people. His ideas helped poor farmers have better lives. His story shows the power of learning and helping others.

GEORGE WASHINGTON CARVER

1896
Starts teaching at Tuskegee Institute in Alabama

1921
Speaks to U.S. Congress about the many uses of peanuts

The George Washington Carver Museum at Tuskegee Institute

Carver's picture appeared on a 32-cent U.S. postage stamp in 1998. It was the second stamp with his picture.

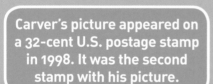

George Washington Carver

32 USA

1998

1943
Dies on January 5

1948
His picture appears on a three-cent U.S. postage stamp

1965
The U.S. Navy names a submarine the U.S.S. *George Washington Carver*

What in the World?

These pictures show up-close views of items from George Washington Carver's time. Use the hints to figure out what's in the pictures. Answers are on page 31.

1

2

HINT: Carver found many uses for this crop.

HINT: The U.S. Navy named two of these in Carver's honor.

Word Bank

mules   berries   books   rocks   ships   peanuts

3

HINT: Carver loved to read but had only one of these as a child.

4

HINT: These animals pulled Carver's wagon classroom.

5

HINT: Carver made paint with these.

6

HINT: Carver collected these on the farm where he grew up.

AGRICULTURE: The science of farming

RACISM: The belief that one group of people is better than another

SLAVE: A person who is owned by another person

SUSTAINABLE: Grown in a way that keeps the soil healthy